I0408905

The Ultimate Home Downsizing Handbook:

What to Save, What to Let Go, and
How to Do It with Ease

Beverly J. Shoemake

All rights reserved. No part of this publication may be reproduced, distributed or transmitted in any form or by any means, including photocopying, recording, or other electronic or mechanical methods without the prior written permission of the publisher, except in the case of brief quotations embodied in critical reviews and certain other non-commercial uses permitted by Copyright law.

Copyright © (Beverly J. Shoemake), (2023)

Table of content

Introduction

With the help of "The Ultimate Home Downsizing Handbook," learn about the transforming impact of deliberate living. Are you aching to purge your home of clutter and adopt a more straightforward existence? This thorough manual is the key to opening up a world of opportunities. Enter a journey that goes beyond simple organization and explores what is most important.

You'll learn the art of downsizing in this intelligently written book, focusing on what to save and what to let go. Explore a range of techniques, from confidently tackling each region of your home to sorting techniques for specific goods. Be able to gracefully navigate emotional attachments, handle sentimental belongings with care, and master the freeing act of guilt-free letting go.

However, downsizing isn't just about stuff; it's also about creating a life that supports your ideals. Discover innovative storage options that make the most of limited space and enjoy the delight of living an orderly, clutter-free life. Learn how to manage your virtual clutter and organize your online activities for more balance and focus.

You won't have to tackle the difficulty of moving to a simpler lifestyle alone. This manual is your dependable travel companion since it offers helpful guidance on moving, settling into a smaller place, and adapting to a minimalist lifestyle. Create a home that reflects your goals and purposes rather than merely being a place for you to live.

With long-term success techniques that make sure your smaller lifestyle flourishes, maintain your newfound simplicity. Enjoy the advantages of lower stress, improved wellbeing, and financial independence. You'll learn the important fact that living a life free of clutter creates more joy, space, and room for what matters most.

The book "*The Ultimate Home Downsizing Handbook*" is more than just a book; it's a life-changing experience that gives you the power to change your surroundings, your perspective, and your way of living. Accept the beauty of accepting what really matters and the liberation that comes from letting go. Begin today on the path to a life that is easier and more meaningful.

Chapter 1

Embracing the Downsizing Journey

Downsizing may seem contradictory in a culture that frequently promotes acquisition and excess. However, the idea has the power to profoundly alter not only our living quarters but also our lives. Making conscious decisions that are in line with what is most important to us is an important part of the downsizing process rather than just getting rid of things.

We set out on a journey of learning and transformation in this chapter. We cordially welcome you to alter your viewpoint, reconsider your priorities, and investigate the empowering practice of letting go. You'll discover tips, tricks, and motivation in the pages that follow to help you deal with the complexities of downsizing with assurance and grace.

Are you prepared to make room for what matters most? Let's explore the world of downsizing and open the doors to a more straightforward, purposeful way of life.

- Benefits of Simplifying Your Life

I think most of us would agree that simplifying and decluttering our houses has many advantages. I want to discuss some of the more unforeseen advantages of simplification today.
We anticipate more time and room.
There are some benefits of decluttering that we expect and anticipate when we start doing it in our houses. For instance, when we eliminate the clutter from our lives, we anticipate having more time and space.
Because there is less stuff when the clutter is cleared, our homes naturally have more room.
Because we aren't spending as much time looking for, picking up, cleaning, organizing, looking for, fixing, picking up again, etc. all the items we already have, we have more time. Simplifying has several advantages, including the simple fact that you won't lose items and

won't have to spend as much time and effort hunting for them.

Some advantages of simplification are more unexpected.

I've been decluttering, simplifying, and residing in our clutter-free house for well over 8 years at this point. I adore the additional time and space that simplifying has afforded my entire family and me.But I've found that simplicity has many more advantages than I initially thought.

I started decluttering our home because I was tired of finding the same "stuff" everywhere and I realized we didn't need or utilize all of it. My intention was to streamline the cleaning process so that I could spend less time maintaining our home and more time enjoying it. I've been able to accomplish all of that and so much more by simplifying and decluttering our home and lives.

With less stuff, cleaning and maintaining a neat home is so much simpler! Less "stuff" needs to be picked up and cleaned up around. There will also be less clutter to clean! But there have been considerably more benefits to simplifying our life and house. I want to share with you some advantages of simplifying right now that I didn't anticipate when I initially started trying to get rid of the clutter. And what a pleasant surprise these advantages have been!

1. More contentment at home

One fantastic advantage of decluttering and simplifying your home is that you'll feel happy and content there.

You not only make extra room in your home when you get rid of clutter. But you also contribute to increasing happiness and appreciation for the house you already have.

Maybe all you need is less stuff to occupy your space instead of a bigger home or more storage.

Additionally, a home that isn't overrun with "stuff" that consumes your time, space, and energy feels less stressful and takes up less of your time. Your home may be cleaned, organized, and maintained considerably more easily.

Additionally, it's simple to use, store, and locate each object you decide to keep when you have a specific location for it.

2. Improved connections

This has been a great unanticipated benefit of simplifying, and I definitely wasn't anticipating decluttering to have such a big impact on my relationships!

You have more time and energy to devote to your relationships with the people you love when your home and your "stuff" take up less of your time and energy.

Your home and your "stuff" won't demand as much of your attention and focus, allowing you to devote more of it to your friends and family. And those relationships can develop and get deeper when you can put your time and effort into them with the people you love the most!

Additionally, if you live in a house that is simpler to maintain and keep clean, you'll probably experience less stress and hostility toward your family because you won't feel as though there is always something to do or a chaotic mess to deal with. And one excellent strategy to create the chance to enhance your interactions with your family is to get rid of any sources of persistent worry or resentment.

3. More joy and endurance

The change in my attitude that came about as a result of downsizing our home was one of the most unexpected advantages. Until it was gone, I was unaware of how stressed out all the "stuff" in our house had made me.

I felt overwhelmed and irritable when our house was cluttered, disorganized, and chaotic. I already felt exhausted by how much time and energy our home and "stuff" required of me, so I wouldn't have much patience. To feel calm and tranquil, I need order in our house.

It was such an easy fix to just get rid of whatever we didn't use or need.

Even now, when I'm cleaning and taking care of the house, if I ever feel irritable or anxious, that's typically a clue that I need to perform another fast round of decluttering.

4. Less worry

According to studies, clutter can make people feel stressed out and anxious.

Additionally, clutter can overstimulate your brain, resulting in stress and making it challenging to unwind. A lot of worry and anxiety can also be brought on by the impending ideas of everything you need to do, including clean up, find stuff, take care of your home, etc.

Life might feel out of control when your home is messy, disordered, and out of order, which can cause tension and anxiety. We may eliminate a big source of stress from our homes and lives, as well as reduce anxiety, by simplifying and decluttering.

Even your sleep might be improved by clearing up the clutter in your home. Your brain has the opportunity to unwind, relax, and sleep better in a space that is clutter-free.

5. Financial independence and more money

You have chosen to own fewer things when you decide to declutter and simplify. And you typically buy less when you decide to own fewer things. This not only helps you save money, but it also increases your financial flexibility.

As you start making purchases with more thinking and intention, your spending habits get better. And once you start to recognize you have enough, you frequently wind up buying less overall.

You have the freedom to spend your money on the things that are essential to you when your spending habits become more deliberate.

6. Reduced shopping

In addition to saving you money, simplification has the wonderful and unexpected bonus of making you shop less.

How much time do you devote to doing errands, shopping, contemplating purchases, contemplating purchases, researching purchases, etc.?

You decide to buy less when you decide to own less. And this liberates a significant amount of time and energy that was previously spent consuming and purchasing additional "stuff"!

Instead, you may decide to invest your time and effort in something that will benefit you more in the long run. similar to engaging in a passion project or spending time with the people you cherish. All of this without having to subsequently clean, organize, gather, search for, take care of, etc. of the clutter in your home!

7. More freedom and enjoyable opportunities
You give yourself more freedom and possibilities to have fun when you spend less time managing all the "stuff" you own.
Knowing that you won't get behind on domestic duties or end up paying for it later because your home will be out of control allows you to say yes more often. simply because once there is less stuff, your home won't require as much of your attention.
"Less things equal less mess.
More time equals less mess.
Time + freedom = freedom.
thanks to Janine Young

8. More self-assurance

Your confidence might rise if your house is in order in a way that makes you feel at ease, pleased, and content. Instead of your house controlling you, it feels the opposite way around. It helps you feel accomplished, which boosts your confidence and makes you feel good.

In our consumer-driven culture, living with less can occasionally feel counter-cultural. However, you feel confident in your decision to simplify your home now that you are aware of the advantages of simplification for improving your happiness and health.

When you simplify and tidy your home, you could even feel more eager to invite guests and family. You could be more willing to extend an invitation to someone into your home if you feel secure and content with it rather than embarrassed by the mess. Which only serves to strengthen your relationships going forward!

9. Being more mindful in your life

You tend to become more aware of where your time and attention are going when you simplify and declutter your house and life. If your time and attention are going in the direction you want them to, you will be better equipped to make conscious decisions. By practicing mindfulness, you may be more in the now throughout the day rather than getting sidetracked by your "stuff" and the time and effort it consumes.

Additionally, living for the present rather than dwelling on the past or worrying about the future is made possible by simplifying and decluttering. Decluttering can help you stop thinking about every conceivable future possibility and instead focus on what you use and need right now, in the present. For instance, instead of storing things "just in case" you might need them "someday," you can stop keeping things "just in case" you might need them "someday".

Additionally, clearing out your environment allows you to let go of the past and make room for the person you are now.

It's nice to have some sentimental mementos from the past. However, if there are too many sentimental artifacts, they lose their particular, important status and become a clutter-causing mess. When your home is filled with mementos from the past, it's difficult to live in the present.

You can let go of worries and fears about the future as well as break free from living in the past by cleaning up and simplifying your home. All of this is done to allow you to enjoy the present and who you are right now.

10. Make experiences more valuable than "things"

The way simplifying alters your perspective to put more emphasis on what you can do rather than what you can buy is another unexpected benefit.

You begin to understand that all the "stuff" you accumulate will eventually become the junk you spend your time and energy organizing, cleaning, finding, and picking up, among other things.

Instead of adding additional "stuff" to your life and house to maintain or clutter, experiences allow you to create memories, have fun, and so on.

11. Extra appreciation

This has to be the most significant benefit of all the unexpected ones that simplification offers.

You have more time and energy to value and appreciate what you do have when you have less possessions.

Because it enhances your quality of life, you realize that what you have is sufficient. When you value what you own because you use and love it, it is simpler to appreciate what you have. Instead of being a chore that consumes more time and effort than it is worth.

In addition, you begin to appreciate what you already have as your perspective changes from desiring to acquire more and more.

Chapter 2

The Downsizing Mindset

Welcome to a chapter that explores the core of the downsizing process in depth. In this article, we'll look at the transformative potential of a downsizing mindset, a style of thinking that enables you to let go of the pointless and embrace a simpler, more purposeful life.

The mental patterns and ideas that may have kept you bound to excess goods will be examined in this chapter, along with techniques for escaping them. By changing your viewpoint, you'll open the door to a new beginning that is consistent with your genuine objectives and values.

Prepare to examine the current quo and traditional notions of success as well as the opportunities that present themselves once you let go of the need for "more" and make place for a more real life.

- Shifting Perspectives for a Fresh Start

The idea of changing perspectives toward a new beginning through downsizing may be both revolutionary and liberating in a world that frequently praises accumulation and the never-ending search of more. In today's society, the pull of having more things, bigger houses, and grander lifestyles is ingrained. But when people struggle with stress, anxiety, and a lack of genuine fulfillment, the allure of a simpler, more deliberate existence becomes more and more appealing.

Reassessing Happiness and Success

Reassessing our definitions of success and happiness is the first step in changing our perceptions for a new beginning. Success has always been associated with material prosperity, lofty positions, and the desire for approval from others. However, this frequently results in a cycle of never-ending striving, leaving us with a sense of constant unhappiness.

We question the traditional definition of success by embracing downsizing. We understand that pursuing a successful job or amassing a large collection of material items won't always lead to true happiness. Instead, it's about developing deep relationships, taking part in enjoyable activities, and living a life that is consistent with our underlying values.

Getting Rid of Extras

A desire to let go of the excess that clogs our life is necessary to change perspectives in the direction of a new beginning. From the physical clutter in our houses to the cerebral clutter brought on by overcommitment and information overload, this excess can take many different forms.

Physically, decluttering is choosing carefully what we surround ourselves with. It's about realizing that each item you own has a price tag attached to it, not only financially but also in terms of the time and effort it takes to maintain and manage it. We make room for what really matters by letting go of things that don't make us happy or serve a purpose.

Prioritizing our responsibilities and concentrating on activities that support our aims and values are key components of mental cleaning. This could entail limiting the amount of time we spend digesting information from diverse sources or saying "no" to additional obligations that sap our vitality. We may build a sense of clarity and present in our daily lives by clearing our minds of mental clutter.

Developing an Attitude of Abundance

The change from a scarcity mindset to an abundance mindset is among the most significant shifts in perspective that come with downsizing. The worry of not having enough, whether in terms of resources like time, opportunity, or belongings, is the hallmark of a scarcity mindset. This way of thinking can cause feelings of worry, rivalry, and persistent lack.

A worldview of wealth, on the other hand, recognizes the intrinsic richness of our existence. It acknowledges that our value isn't determined exclusively by our goods or accomplishments. We can access a world of opportunities by emphasizing our gratitude for what we have, whether it is our health, relationships, or personal strengths.

The act of letting go becomes empowering rather than anxiety-inducing when we switch to an abundance attitude. We come to understand that by letting go of what no longer serves us, we make room in our life for fresh encounters, connections, and chances.

Building Resilience in a Changing World

Perspective-shifting for a new beginning through downsizing necessitates accepting change and developing resilience in the face of uncertainty. The idea of letting go of familiar objects or habits might cause emotions of uneasiness. Change can can bring about a mix of emotions, ranging from anticipation to fear.

However, downsizing offers a special chance to build resilience, the capacity to adjust and prosper in the face of difficulty. We develop the ability to embrace discomfort and see it as a driver for growth as we work through the difficulties of downsizing. We improve our capacity for flexibility, open-mindedness, and graceful transition.

Accepting Authenticity and Goals

In the end, adopting authenticity and purpose is what it really means to alter perspectives for a new beginning. It's about making decisions that reflect who we really are and what we really value. We make room to explore our passions and engage in activities that make us happy as we let go of societal expectations and outside influences.

This quest for authenticity necessitates reflection and self-awareness. It requires self-reflection on what is genuinely important, what fulfills us, and how we want to make a difference in the world. We not only feel a deep feeling of fulfillment when we live in accordance with our real selves, but we also motivate others to do the same.

Perspective-shifting for a new beginning by downsizing is a transforming journey that pushes us to question the current quo, reevaluate our values, and embrace a more straightforward, purposeful way of living. It involves getting rid of the excess that drags us down and making way for the things that really make our lives richer.

Downsizing is not just about reducing our physical surroundings; it's also about living a life that reflects our genuine selves as we rethink our ideas of success and happiness, let go of the excess, create an abundant mindset, and accept change and authenticity.

We discover strength, fortitude, and the ability to live freely on this path. By changing our viewpoints, we set out on a journey to a new beginning that is not only enlightening for ourselves but also beneficial for our communities and the environment.

- Overcoming Change Resistance

Even though change is a necessary part of life, we frequently experience resistance to it. Discomfort, worry, and even panic might be induced by the idea of leaving behind old routines, habits, and things. Overcoming aversion to change becomes a crucial step towards embracing a more intentional and happy lifestyle in the context of changing perceptions for a new beginning through downsizing.

Understanding Resistance's Nature

Our innate demand for stability and security is the core of resistance to change as a psychological reaction. Because the perceived hazards associated with the unfamiliar are reduced by the familiar, our brains are built to seek comfort in it. When faced with the possibility of downsizing, this propensity, often known as the "status quo bias," can show up in a number of different ways.

Resistance to change frequently appears as a string of emotional and cognitive responses:

1. dread of Loss: Even if a possession's primary worth is sentimental, getting rid of it might cause a dread of losing something significant or valuable.

2. Uncertainty: It might be unnerving to face the unknown. Moving to a new location, changing your lifestyle, or making unusual decisions may be required while downsizing.

3. Identity Attachment: Our identities frequently entangle with our possessions. It may feel as if we are letting go of a piece of ourselves when we let go of them.

4. Comfort in Familiarity: Being familiar can make something feel safe and predictable. This comfort is upset by change, which causes resistance.

- Mindset Shifts to Beat Resistance

The first step in overcoming aversion to change is to adjust our perspectives and reframe how we view the upcoming changes. The following tips will aid you in completing this journey:

1. **Recognize your emotions:** Recognize and accept the feelings that come up when thinking about reducing. Feeling apprehensive or uncertain is acceptable; these emotions are real.

2. **Concentrate on What You Gain**: Instead of worrying about potential losses, concentrate on the benefits of downsizing, such as extra room, flexibility, or a simpler way of life.

3. **Contest Unfavorable Beliefs**: Determine the unfavorable ideas that support resistance and

confront them. Consider challenging beliefs like, "I need to keep everything to be happy."

4. **Develop a Vision**: Picture the advantages of shrinking. Imagine the environment you'll build, the adventures you'll have, and the sensation of freedom you'll have.

5. **Break Down the reducing process into doable, smaller phases.** This can help the adjustments seem more manageable and less overwhelming.

6. **Put Self-Compassion into Practice:** Throughout the procedure, be kind to yourself. It's acceptable to experience some uncertainty during the process of change.

Accepting Change as a Chance for Growth
Although resistance to change is common, it's important to understand that it also offers an opportunity for personal development and transformation. By accepting new experiences and moving beyond of our comfort zones, we broaden our horizons and uncover parts of ourselves that may have lain dormant.

The opportunity to develop traits like adaptation, resilience, and courage is provided by downsizing. It challenges us to reassess our goals, make deliberate decisions, and gain a clearer grasp of what is most important to us in life. We acquire emotional intelligence and the ability to accept change in other aspects of our lives as we face opposition and work through it.

Practical Techniques for Combating Resistance

Practical techniques can be used in addition to changing mindsets to get through resistance to change:

1. Have a positive outlook and approach the downsizing process with curiosity and excitement. As opposed to being a difficult task, think of it as an adventure.

2. Establish Clear Intentions: Explain your rationale for downsizing. You'll feel motivated and have a sense of purpose if your aims are clear.

3. Establish a Support System: Talk to friends, relatives, or a support group about your

experience downsizing. A big difference may be made by surrounding yourself with supportive others.

4. Keep Your Eyes on the Present: During the downsizing process, try not to think too much about the difficulties that lie ahead. Practicing mindfulness can reduce anxiety.

5. LCelebrate Progress: Honor even the slightest victories encountered. As you go closer to your downsizing goals, treat yourself.

Recognize that plans may change, and that's good. 6. Exercise Flexibility. Being adaptable enables you to deal with unforeseen circumstances without being overwhelmed.

Getting beyond change-related resistance is a crucial step in the downsizing process. It calls for a combination of altering perspectives, building resilience, and applying useful tactics. We can overcome the difficulties of downsizing with more ease and confidence by comprehending the nature of resistance, altering our perceptions, and accepting change as an opportunity for progress.

We create the foundation for a more intentional and satisfying way of life when we learn to let go of attachments, embrace uncertainty, and step beyond of our comfort zones. In the end, overcoming aversion to change not only changes our physical surroundings but also sparks personal development and gives us the ability to live more honestly.

Identifying What Really Matters in

Chapter 3

Identifying What Truly Matters

Identifying what is really important in your life is the core of downsizing, and this chapter will help you accomplish just that. The act of taking the time to identify your necessities is an act of reclaiming your priorities and altering your path towards a more conscious and fulfilling existence in a world that constantly bombards us with messages of materialism and the quest of more.

This chapter will discuss the skill of discernment, which is the process of identifying the things, pursuits, and connections that enhance your wellbeing and are consistent with your values. You will get insight into the areas of your life that merit your time, energy, and attention via introspection and deliberate review.

- Uncovering Your Essentials

The process of identifying your necessities emerges as a beacon of clarity amid the confusion in a society that is constantly bombarded with information, things, and options. A journey of discernment is an art that calls for self-reflection, mindfulness, and a profound understanding of your beliefs and objectives. It entails determining what matters most in your life and setting those priorities.

In a Materialistic Culture, What Are the Essentials?

The idea of basics has a deeper meaning in a society where things are frequently associated with success and happiness. Essentials aren't simply things you can't live without; they're also things that improve your wellbeing, support your values, and give your life meaning.

Material goods can contribute to this, but they are only one factor. Your connections, interests, pursuits, and the way you spend your time and energy are all essential. The process of identifying your necessities allows you to look beyond worldly needs and investigate the fundamental elements that genuinely improve your life.

The Influence of Reflection

Introspection, a process of self-examination that entails digging into your ideas, feelings, desires, and motives, is the first step in discovering your basics. Understanding what actually resonates with you and what can be the result of outside influences or cultural expectations requires a purposeful inward turn.

Consider posing the following questions to yourself while you reflect:

- What gives me the most happiness and fulfillment?
- What pursuits cause me to become time-disoriented?
- Who are the folks who inspire and encourage me?
- What principles do I uphold, and how may I live my life in accordance with them?

You'll start to discover patterns and preferences through introspection that lead you to a better knowledge of your core values.

Keeping Your Values in Mind

The congruence with your values is the cornerstone of discovering your essentials. Your values act as a compass to help you make decisions, establish priorities, and choose what you believe is most important. When you give priority to the things that are most important to you and that align with your values, your life becomes authentic and congruent.

Think about your essential values, whether they be courage, creativity, adventure, or something else entirely. You'll gain awareness of the areas of your life that demand your focus and investment as you pinpoint these principles. For instance, if spending time with family and friends is a core value, cultivating relationships becomes crucial to your journey.

Eliminating Non-Essentials

Losing non-essentials that clutter your life is frequently a necessary step in discovering your essentials. This can include material goods, obligations, and even attitudes that are no longer beneficial to you. Decluttering your environment, whether it is your actual space or your mental landscape, makes place for the things that are really important.

Accept the process of decluttering as powerful. Consider it an opportunity to create room for development, creativity, and calmness rather than seeing it as a loss. You'll feel liberated as you let go of non-essentials and develop a fresh appreciation for the things and events that add meaning to your life.

Putting Your Time and Energy in Order

Finding your fundamentals requires conscious time and energy management as well. The way you choose to use your limited time reveals your priorities. Think about the pursuits that feed your spirit, improve your wellbeing, and advance your development as a person.

This doesn't mean getting rid of all tedious or important work; rather, it means finding a balance between duties and pursuits that are in line with your priorities. You can achieve peace and avoid the feeling of being continually tugged in multiple ways by purposefully arranging your time and energy.

Making a Decision-Making Framework

You will create a framework for decision-making that is in line with your beliefs and objectives as you go through the process of identifying your fundamentals. When faced with options, whether they are related to purchases, commitments, or life-changing decisions, this framework becomes a useful tool.

When faced with a choice, think about how it fits with your priorities. Does it fit with your morals? Does it improve your well-being in any way? Does it help you live the life you're consciously building? You are given the ability to make decisions using this framework that are in line with your actual priorities.

Finding your fundamentals involves a path of self-discovery, mindfulness, and deliberate living. It's a process that pushes you to break free from societal expectations, connect with your beliefs, and design a life that fulfills your highest desires.

As you proceed on this journey, keep in mind that identifying your basics is a continuous process that changes as you learn and experience more. You set out on a journey to a life that is truly yours through introspection, alignment with values, letting go of non-essentials, prioritizing time and energy, and developing a framework for decision-making.

By identifying your basics, you build a solid basis for a life of meaning, fulfillment, and real connection—a life that is in line with your heart's actual goals and makes a good difference in the world.

- Assessing Your Needs vs. Wants

The art of separating your requirements from your wants is one of the essential ideas that might help you navigate the process of downsizing the family home. Cultivating this judgment is essential to making a home that reflects your genuine goals and improves your quality of life in a society where necessity and want are frequently conflated.

Specifying Wants and Needs

Establishing a firm knowledge of needs and wants is crucial before starting the evaluation process. The fundamental components needed for a comfortable and useful life are needs. These are the factors that directly affect your health, safety, and fundamental functioning. Contrarily, wants are longings that go above and beyond the basics and add to your delight, pleasure, and individual preferences.

Assessing your requirements versus wants while downsizing entails looking at the things, places, and activities that make up your everyday routine.

Embracing Intentional Living and Minimalism

The idea of evaluating your requirements against wants is quite similar to minimalism and deliberate living. While purposeful living urges us to make decisions that are in line with our beliefs and objectives, minimalism encourages us to get rid of excess and concentrate on what really important. Both ideas place a higher value on experiences than things and emphasize quality over quantity.

You'll be able to recognize the possessions that actually serve a purpose and provide value to your life through the assessment procedure. With the help of this technique, you may design a home that enhances your wellbeing, clears the clutter, and promotes peace.

The Technique of Let-Go

One of the most transforming components of downsizing is learning the art of letting go. When you let go, you let go of attachments to things that no longer serve your needs, values, or aspirations. To engage in this practice, one must be prepared to let go of the past and accept the present.

A well-organized foundation for letting go is provided by evaluating your requirements against wants. When presented with an item, consider whether it truly fills a need in your life or if it is just a want. *Does it improve my well-being or just create more clutter?*

Establishing a Complete Inventory

Consider making a thorough inventory of your belongings and areas so that you can compare your necessities and wants. This list gives you a visual depiction of your possessions and enables you to assess each one fairly.

Create categories for your inventory, such as apparel, gadgets, furniture, and sentimental goods. Identify which goods fall into each category as "needs" or "wants." When making an assessment, be sincere and unbiased. Items that no longer serve their intended purpose or are consistent with your values can be classified as "wants."

Functionality and utility should come first

By weighing your needs and wants, you're encouraged to give practicality and utility in your living space priority. Pay attention to things that improve your daily life and have a practical use. Think on how each item affects your routines, pursuits, and general wellbeing.

Consider the furniture's practicality and how it fits into your lifestyle, for instance, while evaluating it. Is the furniture useful and comfy, or is it only ornamental and rarely used? You may design a room that is effective, orderly, and meets your needs by giving practical elements top priority.

Matching Your Lifestyle

Aligning your things with your existing lifestyle is another consideration when determining requirements versus wants. The things that once satisfied our requirements may be out of date because our lives are continually changing. Consider each item in the context of your current way of life and everyday activities when evaluating it.

Think about your interests, activities, and hobbies. Do your assets contribute to and improve these facets of your life, or are they merely artifacts from earlier endeavors? You can construct a home that supports your present interests and objectives by matching your stuff to your way of life.

Sentimental items are the Emotional Aspect.
It's especially important to weigh necessities and wishes when it comes to sentimental goods. The decision to let go is made more difficult since sentimental items frequently have emotional worth and memories attached to them. When evaluating sentimental goods, pay attention to the emotional value they have for you.

Choose a few items that have the most profound meaning rather than holding on to every sentimental item. Think about digitizing pictures, making memory boxes, or coming up with subtle ways to add sentimental artifacts to your home without overwhelming it. By using this technique, you can prioritize your basic necessities while still paying tribute to your memories.

Assessing your requirements versus wants is a habit that goes beyond evaluating your material items; it permeates every step of your downsizing process. You may create a home that is thoughtful, peaceful, and representative of your values by separating wants from needs.

Keep in mind that determining your needs versus wants is an ongoing process as you move through this process. Your needs and desires could change over time, and that's quite normal. You set out on a route to a smaller house that celebrates the essence of what really important through reflection, letting go, emphasizing functionality, fitting with your lifestyle, and addressing the emotional side.

In the end, learning how to distinguish between your requirements and wants gives you the power to create a home that makes you happy, improves your wellbeing, and aids in your transition to intentional living.

Chapter 4

Strategies for Efficient Decluttering

Hello and welcome to this chapter on the useful and transformational process of decluttering. Decluttering becomes a cornerstone of the downsizing process as a way to make room in the physical and mental realms for what is actually important. This chapter provides a thorough explanation of how to use efficient sorting techniques for a variety of items, enabling you to move through the decluttering process with assurance and comfort.

Every item you own, from clothing to sentimental things, has a story to tell, and by decluttering your home, you can create a space that reflects your values and objectives. In this chapter, we'll look at methods for empowering you to make wise choices, give priority to necessities, and start living intentionally by learning the art of decluttering.

- Sorting Methods for Various Items

The act of decluttering emerges as a crucial stage in the aim of downsizing and building a home that reflects your true priorities. Decluttering is a purposeful approach that involves evaluating your stuff, making educated decisions, and curating a space that reflects your beliefs. It's not just about getting rid of extra things. This chapter provides a thorough examination of decluttering techniques that are suitable for a variety of objects, settings, and situations.

Decluttering: The Art of Going Beyond Minimalism

Beyond the minimalist style, clearing out clutter is a good idea. You can dynamically match your assets to your priorities, lifestyle, and personal development through this method. You free up space for what really counts by getting rid of things that are no longer useful, both physically and mentally.

Think of your belongings as a record of your life's adventure. Decluttering makes it possible for you to put together a collection that offers a significant tale because every thing has a backstory. Each category, from clothing and accessories to sentimental objects and home goods, demands a different strategy for properly decluttering.

Clothing and accessory purging

It may be both liberating and difficult to organize your wardrobe and accessories. Many times, memories, goals, and emotional relationships are carried in clothing. Think about the following tactics when you approach your wardrobe:

1. **The KonMari Method**: Made popular by Marie Kondo, this technique has you hold each object and ask yourself if it makes you happy. It's time to let it go if it doesn't.

2. **One-In-One-Out Rule:** Make a commitment to getting rid of one existing thing for every new item you bring in. This discourages

accumulation and promotes consumption that is deliberate.

3. Seasonal Rotation: Only keep items of clothing that are suitable for the present season. To keep a manageable and carefully maintained collection, rotate pieces as the seasons change.

Getting Rid of Emotional Items

It can be hard to purge sentimental items because they have a special place in our hearts. However, the sentiment associated with these goods doesn't always dwell in the actual object. Think about the following techniques for handling sentimental clutter:

1. The Memory Box: Designate a memory box where you can retain a select few nostalgic objects with the greatest personal significance.

2. Photographic Preservation: To keep memories without taking up physical space, digitize photos, letters, and other mementos.

3. Selected Display: Pick just a few precious things to put on display in your home so you can pay tribute to their value without overcrowding the space.

Cleaning Up the Home Goods

The term "household goods" refers to a broad range of products, including cookery and ornamental items. Getting rid of these things will improve your home's usefulness and appearance:

1. Functional Assessment: Consider the functionality of each piece of domestic equipment. Consider getting rid of something that is rarely utilized or has a redundant purpose.

2. Reliance on Usability Over Beauty Give practical goods more importance than those that are just decorative. An atmosphere devoid of clutter is facilitated by functional goods.

3. Organizing by Room: To avoid being overwhelmed, divide the decluttering effort per room. Concentrate on a single topic at a time to ensure a thorough and organized approach.

Digital purging

In the modern world, decluttering includes your online presence. Your focus and productivity may be affected by digital clutter, which can be just as distracting as physical clutter. Think about the following digital cleaning techniques:

1. Email and Inbox Management: Unsubscribe from irrelevant emails, sort key emails into categories, and routinely empty your inbox.

2. Arrange Digital Files: Create structured folders for files, eliminate duplication, and archive outdated papers.

3. Perform a social media audit of your accounts, unfollowing or muzzling those that do not reflect your interests or values.

The Pareto Principle: The Influence of the 80/20 Rule

According to the Pareto Principle, or 80/20 rule, 80% of effects result from 20% of causes. When it comes to decluttering, it implies that a sizable amount of your possessions might not make a major difference in your life. You can recognize and concentrate on the things that have the biggest influence thanks to this idea.

Effective decluttering techniques are founded in focus, mindfulness, and a profound comprehension of your requirements versus wants. Keep in mind that decluttering is a continuous process as you work through the process of getting rid of your clothes, accessories, sentimental objects, household items, and digital places. It is a continuing activity that supports the development of your values and way of life.

By putting these tactics into practice, you start a transformational journey that not only improves your home's outward appearance but also fosters mental clarity, focus, and wellbeing. By purging your life of unnecessary items, aligning it with your goals, and fostering a stronger connection to what really matters, you can create a life that prioritizes the necessities.

- Tackling Different Areas of Your Home

One of the best methods to use as you start your path of decluttering is to go through your home one room at a time. Every room has its own particular set of items, difficulties, and potential for change. By taking a thorough approach to decluttering, you establish a peaceful living space that is in line with your beliefs, improves your wellbeing, and encourages deliberate living.

The Living Room: Creating a Calm and Comfortable Environment

The living room is frequently the center of the house; here, family members and friends can gather to unwind and entertain. Take into account the following methods to successfully clear this space:

1. Furniture and Layout: Examine your living room's furniture to make sure each piece is functional. Organize the furnishings to encourage conversation and movement.

2. Decorative and Emotional Items: Choose a few noteworthy accents and arrange them tastefully. To avoid visual clutter, keep the quantity of ornamental items to a minimum.

3. Media and Electronics: Arrange your book, DVD, and video game collections. Reduce the amount of devices on show to create a calmer environment.

Streamlining for Efficiency in the Kitchen

Efficiency and organization are key in the kitchen, a functioning hub. Consider using the following techniques to organize this area:

1. Utensils and Appliances: Examine your devices, appliances, and utensils. Consider keeping the things you use frequently and selling or donating the duplicates or infrequently used things.

2. Check expiration dates on food in the refrigerator and pantry on a regular basis and throw away anything that is no longer fit for consumption. Organize your refrigerator and pantry for quick access to ingredients.

3. Keep cookware and serveware that are compatible with your cooking style. Donate anything you don't use very often or that's taking up too much space.

Making a Calm Haven in the Bedroom

Your bedroom is your own haven, a place for rest and renewal. Better sleep and peace of mind can be fostered by clearing the clutter from your bedroom:

1. Clothes and Accessories : Organize your closet using decluttering techniques like the KonMari Method or the one-in-one-out rule. Make your closet organized so you can find your favorite stuff quickly.

2. Beside the Bed: Don't let your bedside table become overly cluttered. Pick a few things that help you unwind, such a book or a calming lamp.

3. Storage Options : Take full advantage of storage options to keep personal items tidy and hidden. Think about wall-mounted shelves or under-the-bed storage.

The Restroom: Self-Care Made Simple

The bathroom is a place for daily rituals and self-care. Place an emphasis on functionality and simplicity when clearing this space:

1. Toiletries and other items: Go through your products and toiletries. Throw away everything that has expired or is no longer in use. Think about limiting your purchases to necessities.

2. Towels and Linens: Keep a sufficient number of the towels and linens you use frequently. Old or infrequently used objects should be recycled or donated.

3. Prescription drugs and first aid: Verify the expiration dates on your medications frequently, and properly discard anything that has passed its expiration date. For quick access, arrange your first aid and pharmaceutical supplies.

Home Office: Increasing Concentration and Productivity

A place for work, creativity, and productivity is the home office. This space can be decluttered to improve focus and foster a positive working environment:

1. Desk and Workspace: Arrange your paperwork and supplies to keep your desk clear of clutter. To manage stationery and tiny stuff, think about utilizing organizers and bins.

2. Technology and Cables: To avoid tangles and clutter, organize cables and chargers. Eliminate extraneous electronics or devices that provide visual distraction.

3. Storage and Filing : Create a systemized filing system for paperwork and documents. Important documents should be digitalized to reduce physical clutter.

You can create a living environment that supports your well-being, values, and objectives by systematically decluttering various sections of your home. The living room, kitchen, bedroom, bathroom, and home office may all be made more practical, orderly, and inviting by decluttering them.

Keep in mind that decluttering is about establishing a harmonious environment for your life's journey, not just getting rid of things. Every room in your house has the capacity to change, serving as a blank canvas on which you can create a life that resonates with ease, direction, and clarity.

You set out on a transformative journey that goes beyond the physical world by making deliberate decisions and practicing mindful organization. By purging various parts of your home, you lay the groundwork for a life that puts an emphasis on the necessities, promotes wellbeing, and strengthens your connection to what really matters.

Chapter 5

Navigating Emotional Attachments

This chapter explores the emotional landscape of decluttering, which is a space where memories, attachments, and the human experience come together. Navigating emotional ties becomes a profound exploration of our relationships to our goods as well as the skill of striking a balance between the desire for space and simplicity and our fondest memories.

The two key topics covered in this chapter are how to handle sentimental belongings with care and how to let rid of things without feeling guilty. You'll learn how to respect your memories, declutter your home, and embrace the freedom that comes with getting rid of things that are no longer useful as you negotiate the tricky terrain of emotions connected to stuff.

- Handling Sentimental Items with Care

The emotional terrain of sentimental goods might be one of the trickiest to travel during the process of cleaning and downsizing. These things are filled with experiences, narratives, and feelings that have impacted our life. Respecting the past while making room for a more intentional and clutter-free future involves a careful balance when handling sentimental artifacts. Consider these techniques for elegantly managing the emotional difficulties of treasured possessions as you start your journey of decluttering.

Sentiment: Feelings expressed through objects

Sentimental objects have the amazing ability to physically capture feelings. They serve as portals to the past, bringing back memories and feelings connected to major events, people, and locations in life. Every object, from letters and photos to heirlooms and memories, has a special story that speaks to us on a very deep level.

Our natural urge to preserve material mementos of special occasions gives rise to the emotional attachment to sentimental objects. However, as we begin the process of decluttering, it's crucial to strike a balance between keeping these treasured memories and the requirement for a home that supports our current lifestyle and future hope.

The Process of Managing Emotional Attachments

You can successfully handle the emotional bonds related to sentimental goods by taking a thoughtful and intentional approach to handling them. Here is a strategy for approaching this procedure:

1. Acknowledge the Emotional Impact: Be aware of the emotional impact these things have for you. Recognize that it's perfectly normal to feel a connection to objects that trigger memories and feelings.

2. Examine each sentimental item separately to determine its significance. Consider why you

value this object and what memories or feelings it brings up for you. Think about how its relevance fits into your current life and core values.

3. Understanding that letting go of a sentimental item does not remove the memories or feelings connected to it will help you to let go of it. The core of those encounters still resides within of you; the object itself is not the only place where those emotions can be stored.

4. Recognize that you can't keep every sentimental object without overcrowding your home and adding unnecessary clutter to your life. Decide what truly matters. Pick things that are most meaningful to you and enhance your sense of wellbeing and pleasure.

Choosing Carefully: Curating Memories

The art of curating sentimental artifacts enables you to build a meaningful collection while keeping your room clutter-free. The following tips can assist you in selecting your collection:

1. Choose a few sentimental artifacts to exhibit in your home with intention. In this manner, you

can frequently appreciate them and respect their worth without overpowering the surrounding visual surroundings.

2. Rotating Displays: To avoid clutter and keep things looking new, switch out sentimental items that are on display. This method enables you to appreciate various pieces at various times.

3. Establish Dedicated Spaces: Set aside distinct locations or containers for certain sentimental items. Have a box for letters, a shelf for photos, and a case for tiny mementos, for instance.

Digitization: Modern Memory Preservation

With less physical clutter because to technology, emotive memories can be preserved effectively. You can strike a balance between maintaining memories and maintaining a clutter-free living area by digitizing precious items:

1. Scanning Old Photographs and papers: Create digital archives by scanning old photos, letters, and papers. These digital versions save up physical space while preserving memories.

2. Create online photo albums or slideshows that you can see at any time using digital albums and

slideshows. This method of revisiting treasured memories saves space.

3. Keeping Stories: Keep a record of the anecdotes and tales related to sentimental objects. This gives the memories more depth and makes sure that future generations will keep them.

The Art of Saying "Goodbye" and Honoring Memories

A thoughtful and deliberate approach is necessary when letting go of treasured items. It involves remembering the past while releasing yourself from the weight of unnecessary possessions:

1. Express Gratitude: Take a minute to express your gratitude for the memories that a treasured object represents before letting it go. This appreciation recognizes its contribution to your life's path.

2. Treasures to Pass Down: Think about giving treasured objects to family members who will value and cherish them. This makes sure that the memories are still treasured.

3. Repurpose and upcycle nostalgic materials to create useful or aesthetic items. For instance, create a quilt out of old garments or decorate your home with vintage objects.

Making Emotional Resilience a Priority

It's crucial to develop emotional resilience as you negotiate the emotional terrain of handling treasured goods. This entails accepting the feelings that surface while also acknowledging your capacity for growth and adaptation:

1. Give yourself permission to feel; accept the feelings that come up while you purge sentimental belongings. It's acceptable to experience melancholy, nostalgia, or even brief joy.

2. Instead than concentrating on the act of letting go, enjoy the memories and experiences that these objects stand in for.

3. Keep Your Eyes on the Present and the Future: When decluttering, keep in mind that you want to create a space that supports your present and future objectives. You can make place for fresh experiences and chances by getting rid of extra possessions.

Carefully handling precious artifacts is a journey through feelings, memories, and personal development. You can develop a stronger connection to what really matters by weighing the importance of each thing, engaging in selective curation, embracing digitization, and approaching the ritual of letting go carefully. You are establishing a setting for living that is true, deliberate, and healthy.

It's important to keep in mind that the beauty of sentimental goods lies not only in their physical presence but also in the memories and stories they arouse. You are creating a tapestry of memories, encounters, and connections as you set out on this transforming trip that will enhance your life's story. You're making a place where the past and the present coexist peacefully through careful treatment and deliberate choices, enabling you to welcome change while conserving the essence of what has shaped you.

- Letting Go without Guilt

The ability to let go without feeling guilty is one of the most difficult yet freeing things to learn in the complex world of decluttering and downsizing. The emotional burden of guilt frequently surfaces as we work through the process of letting go of possessions—guilt over parting with presents, guilt over letting go of items connected to memories, and guilt over the perceived wastefulness of getting rid of things. But achieving a clutter-free home that reflects your values and objectives requires learning to let go without feeling guilty. This chapter looks at coping mechanisms so you may enjoy the liberating power of letting go of possessions with grace and ease while navigating the emotional path of decluttering.

The Burden of Guilt on the Emotions

The act of decluttering might be hampered by guilt, which can make it emotionally difficult to go with possessions. This shame has several origins:

1. Sentimental items retain memories, making it difficult to let go without feeling as though you are throwing away the events they are related with.

2. Social Expectations: Because it's frequently assumed that goods have value, it can be difficult to consider getting rid of things that you think others might find important.

3. Environmental Concerns: Discarding objects that are still usable can cause guilt due to worries about waste and the environment.

4. presents and Obligations: Receiving presents can make you feel guilty since you could feel forced to keep them even if they don't serve a purpose.

Changing the Viewpoint

It's imperative to change your attitude on belongings and their value in order to let go guilt-free. Think about the following strategies:

1. Value Beyond Materialism: Be aware that objects have value beyond just their physical presence. Even when an item is lost, the memories and experiences it was associated with are still present.

2. Put Yourself First: Put your personal well-being ahead of devotion to material things. Stress reduction, improved attention, and mental clarity are all benefits of a clutter-free environment.

3. Honoring the Gift: When letting go of gifts, pay attention to the thought that went into them rather than the actual item. Even if the gift is released, the act of gifting was intended to spread happiness.

Accept the Idea of Abundance

Adopting an abundance mindset, or the conviction that there is always more than enough, is a prerequisite for letting go guilt-free. Accept the following ideas:

1. Memories abound; they are not restricted to material items. Whether the item is there or not, they are many and exist within you.

2. Opportunities in abundance: By clearing space through decluttering, you make room for new encounters, connections, and personal development.

3. Abundance of Giving: Passing on or donating items enables them to continue performing a purpose while bringing joy and enhancing the lives of others.

The Detachment Freedom

The separation from possessions does not imply the separation from the past or the present. Realizing that things don't determine your value or the worth of your experiences is important:

1. Embrace the Buddhist precept of non-attachment, which holds that material items are fleeting and are not a true source of lasting happiness.

2. Consider decluttering as a method to reclaim your personal space, both inside and outside of your home. This area offers potential for development, creativity, and new possibilities.

3. Release the Burden: Keeping things because of guilt can be a burden. Experience the lightness that comes with letting go when you release the burden.

Techniques for Mindful Decluttering

Use methods that encourage mindfulness and reduce guilt when decluttering:

1. Before getting rid of something, do the thanksgiving ritual by thanking it for the memories it evokes and the function it provided in your life. This ceremony celebrates the object's importance.

2. Donate and Share: By turning the act of letting go into a constructive contribution, giving or sharing stuff with others might help you feel less guilty.

3. Review Your Values: Recall the principles and goals you hold dear. Consider whether retaining the item is consistent with those principles or whether letting it go will improve your wellbeing.

Honor the process

Consider clearing out your space as a celebration of your progress, change, and self-awareness. Celebrate the following:

1. Recognize that your attachment to your goods may have changed during the course of your personal evolution. Letting go is a sign of personal development.

2. Focus on the joy that comes with a clutter-free environment when creating space for joy. Enjoy the extra room you now have for the hobbies and adventures you love.

3. Accept the power of making decisions that are consistent with your current identity and ambitions. Every product that is made public is a deliberate decision toward living a life with greater intention.

A fundamental act of self-compassion, development, and empowerment is letting go without feeling guilty. You can build a space that reflects your beliefs and promotes your wellbeing by altering your perspective, accepting abundance, cultivating detachment, and using mindful practices. The process of decluttering transforms into a liberating adventure that releases you from the emotional burden of your stuff.

Remember to let go of things without feeling guilty as you go through the decluttering process. Each item relinquished and each emotional barrier broken makes this skill stronger. In the end, your goal is to create a living space that resonates with honesty, intentionality, and the freedom to live a life in accordance with your deepest aspirations.

Chapter 6

Creative Storage Solutions

The art of creative storage solutions has become essential to maintaining an ordered and clutter-free living environment in the modern world, where space is frequently at a premium. The challenge is the same whether you live in a modest apartment or a large house: how to maximize your space while keeping your possessions orderly and convenient. This chapter looks into the world of creative storage solutions, providing tips on how to make the most of your available space, organize your house efficiently, and create a sanctuary that is functional and pleasing to the eye.

The Importance of Innovative Storage Options

Storage solutions that are innovative go beyond simple utility. They provide you the chance to make your living areas functional, pleasant, and aesthetically beautiful environments that represent your values and way of life. By utilizing the power of clever storage solutions, you not only foster order but also help to foster a relaxed and stress-free environment. Effective storage has a ripple effect across your house and life, simplifying daily tasks and minimizing clutter.

- Maximizing Space in Small Areas

When it comes to storage, small spaces can call for greater imagination and careful design. Here are some creative suggestions for maximizing space in small spaces:

1. Utilize vertical wall space with shelves, hooks, and wall-mounted organizers to create vertical storage. In addition to maximizing space, vertical storage also draws the eye upward, giving the impression of height.

2. Invest in furniture pieces that serve many purposes, such as beds with built-in drawers or ottomans with concealed storage spaces.

3. Utilize underutilized spaces, such as the area above or under stairwells, to your advantage.

These areas can be converted into useful storage options.

4. Install floating shelves on the walls to display objects while keeping the surfaces clear. Your space gains character this way while yet remaining open.

- Organizational Tips for Every Room

Every space in your house offers different organizational options and problems. Here are some pointers for efficiently organizing diverse spaces:

The living room:

1. Choose furniture with concealed storage, such as coffee tables with drawers or sofas with under-seat storage.

2. Install a floating entertainment center to conserve space on the floor and give the room a contemporary feel.

3. Organize goods like magazines, blankets, and remote controls with the help of chic baskets and containers.

Kitchen:
1. Utensils and cutlery can be organized using drawer dividers to provide simple access and a neat look.
2. For effective pantry organizing, use clear containers for dry products and name the shelves.
3. Pots, pans, and utensils can be hung on wall-mounted racks to free up cabinet space.

Bedroom:
1. Utilize the area under your bed for storage by placing rolling drawers or storage bins there.
2. Jewelry Organization: For a neat and attractive display, hang jewelry from wall-mounted hooks or use a pegboard.
3. Use multi-level hangers to store items like scarves, skirts, and pants to free up closet space.

Bathroom:

1. Shower organizers: Install shelves or hanging caddies in the shower to store toiletries close at hand.
2. *medical Cabinet*: Sort the products in your medical cabinet according to frequency of usage and name the containers.
3. Towel Hooks: To increase towel storage and maintain easy access, use hooks rather than towel bars.

Domestic Office:
1. Floating Desks: For smaller home offices, choose floating desks that fold up when not in use to save room.
2. Cord Management: To keep cords neat and free of tangles, use cable organizers and clips.
3. Utilize vertical file organizers to keep paperwork orderly and away from your workspace.

Entryway:
1. To keep shoes and luggage orderly, install built-in benches with storage sections.

2. Wall-Mounted Hooks: To keep the foyer clutter-free, hang coats, hats, and bags on wall-mounted hooks.

3. Spend money on slender shoe racks to keep the foyer from being cluttered with shoes.

Storage area or a garage
1. Utilize overhead space by using ceiling-mounted storage options for things like bicycles, sporting goods, and holiday decorations.

2. Install pegboards on the walls to hang tools, gardening supplies, and other objects where they can be seen easily.

3. Labeled Bins: To make it simpler to find what you need, store objects in the garage in clear, labeled bins.

Establishing a Balance Between Function and Aesthetics

Effective storage solutions improve functionality while also adding to the aesthetic appeal of your living areas. To create a balance between structure and design, take into account following suggestions:

1. Utilize storage options that go well with your present color scheme and fit in smoothly with your decor.

2. Open shelves: Use open shelves sparingly to display things like books, plants, and decor while keeping the area looking tidy.

3. Minimalism: Adopt a minimalist mindset by periodically clearing up your environment and only keeping things that have value and serve a function.

Creative storage options provide you the power to make your home a calming, well-organized, and visually beautiful place. You may lay the groundwork for deliberate living by utilizing organizational strategies specific to each room and making the most of available space in limited spaces. Effective storage has a cascading effect on your everyday activities, improving your wellbeing, lowering your stress level, and building an environment consistent with your values.

Keep in mind that creative storing is a lifelong endeavor. Adapt your storage options as your demands grow and develop. By incorporating these avant-garde concepts into your house, you're not simply adding storage; you're also establishing a lifestyle that embodies ease, direction, and the flexibility to completely interact with your surroundings.

Chapter 7

Eco-Friendly Disposal Methods

What to do with unwanted belongings takes center stage in the process of downsizing and decluttering. The chapter on eco-friendly disposal techniques in "The Ultimate Home Downsizing Handbook" offers advice on how to get rid of things in an ethical and sustainable way. This chapter examines the value of conscious disposal, introduces the ideas of giving, recycling, and reusing, and illustrates how these deeds are consistent with your desire to lead a more sustainable and responsible lifestyle.

- Donating, Recycling, and Repurposing

Eco-friendly disposal techniques are founded on moral precepts that prioritize cutting down on waste, minimizing environmental effect, and improving society. Consider these pillars as you begin this phase of your downsizing journey:

1. Be aware of your responsibility to preserve resources for future generations and to protect the environment. The health of the world is directly impacted by the disposal decisions you make.

2. Social Impact: Be aware that helping those in need might result from donating and reusing products. You benefit society by increasing the life of your belongings.

3. Minimizing Landfill Waste: Preventing waste from going into landfills is the objective. By deciding on environmentally responsible disposal techniques, you actively endeavor to reduce the amount of waste and its harmful effects.

- Donating: Increasing the Usable Life of Things

Giving away stuff that can still benefit someone else by being donated is a kind approach to pass on possessions. Think about the following when donating:

1. Choosing Donatable Items: Go through your belongings and choose those that are in good condition and could be of use to others. Donations are a common way for household items, clothing, furniture, gadgets, and more to find new homes.

2. When choosing organizations, do your homework and pick respectable ones that share your ideals. Donations are frequently required by charities, thrift stores, shelters, and community organizations.

3. Local Impact: To directly assist your community, choose local nonprofits. Donations can help needy neighbors and advance the community.

4. Tax Benefits: To possibly qualify for tax deductions, keep track of your donations. To learn how donations can help your finances, research the tax laws in your area.

Closing the Loop: Recycling

Recycling is an essential part of ethical waste management. When a product cannot be donated or used again, look into recycling options:

1. Research Local Recycling Facilities: *Various materials call for various recycling procedures. Look for nearby facilities that recycle electronics, paper, plastics, and other materials.

2. Proper Sorting: To guarantee that materials are treated properly, sort them into the appropriate recycling categories. Materials with contamination can make recycling more difficult.

3. Electronics may be recycled to recover valuable materials and stop dangerous waste from ending up in landfills. E-waste recycling programs are available from numerous electronics stores and organizations.

4. Before recycling, see whether there are any upcycling or repurposing options for the item. Repurposing outdated items not only minimizes waste but also displays inventiveness.

Repurposing: Giving Objects New Life
The art of repurposing involves turning worthless objects into useful or attractive items. Accept this innovative strategy:

1. Creative Reimagining: Consider things from a new angle. Old t-shirts can be recycled into reusable shopping bags, and a wooden ladder can be transformed into a bookshelf.

2. Home Decor ideas: Look into DIY ideas to repurpose objects. The possibilities are numerous, from turning ancient bags into coffee tables to utilizing old windows as photo frames.

3. Clothing and Textiles: Create quilts, toss pillows, or even patchwork bags out of old clothing. This strategy lessens textile waste while enhancing sentimental value.

- Sustainable Ways to Discard Unwanted Items

Utilizing environmentally responsible disposal techniques is just one aspect of a greater commitment to sustainable living. Keep in mind these guiding principles as you consider your options for giving, recycling, and repurposing:

1. Intentional Consumption: Reconsider your consumption patterns to avoid gathering things

that could someday need to be disposed of. Make thoughtful selections when you shop.

2. Educate and Inspire: Inform and motivate others by sharing your experience with eco-friendly disposal. Collectively, awareness can have a good impact.

3. Recognize that even little actions can have a significant impact on a broader movement. Each item that is given, recycled, or reused eases the burden on ecosystems and resources.

The need of eco-friendly disposal techniques is emphasized in Chapter 7 of "The Ultimate Home Downsizing Handbook". You have an impact that goes beyond your immediate area when you give, recycle, and re-use things. Your dedication to environmentally friendly disposal is in line with a larger movement to save the environment, assist underserved areas, and encourage responsible behavior. As you start along the path of thoughtful disposal, you're accepting your responsibility to protect the environment and act as a force for good.

Chapter 8

Managing Virtual Clutter

Our lives are shaped by a wide universe of virtual clutter as well as our tangible things in the age of digital plenty. Chapter 8 of "The Ultimate Home Downsizing Handbook" reveals the world of controlling virtual clutter, where the bytes and pixels of your digital existence require the same level of attention as the physical objects in your home. This chapter examines digital downsizing techniques and goes into the art of arranging your digital life to make sure that your pursuit of an intentional and uncluttered living is in harmony with your online presence.

- Digital Downsizing Strategies

1. Evaluating Digital Clutter: Start by taking an inventory of your digital clutter. This contains outdated files, dormant programs,

duplicate images, and emails with no further use.

2. Organizing Files: For your documents, pictures, and other digital stuff, make a clear file structure. Files can be logically categorized using folders and subfolders.

3. Dealing with Duplicate Files: To detect and remove duplicate copies of documents, images, and music files, use duplicate file finders.

4. Unsubscribing and Unfollowing: Remove your name from mailing lists and newsletters that are no longer useful to you. Social media accounts that don't improve your online experience should be unfollowed.

5. Reviewing applications and Programs: Check the applications and programs on your devices on a regular basis. Delete any that you don't need or use anymore.

- Organizing Your Digital Life

1. Setting up folders and labels to organize and archive emails is step one in email management. Use filters to arrange incoming emails and unsubscribe from any subscriptions that aren't necessary.

2. Cloud Storage Organization: Use folders and subfolders to arrange your cloud storage. Only sync and backup the files you actually need.

3. Photo Management: Utilize tools or software to classify and arrange your images. To save space, get rid of duplicate, fuzzy, and pointless pictures.

4. Digital Notebook: Make use of programs for digital note-taking to store and arrange data, concepts, and to-do lists.

5. Password Management: Organize and safeguard your online accounts by using a safe password manager.

6. Set aside time each day to regularly tidy your digital devices. Allocate some time every week or month to purge your digital places.

Digital Downsizing Importance

1. Reduced Stress and overload: Stress and overload can result from a busy digital life. Your internet presence can be streamlined to make it simpler to find what you need.

2. Improved Productivity: A well-organized online workplace boosts output. You take less time looking for documents, emails, and data.

3. Enhanced Security: You can increase your digital security by clearing up your digital clutter. You can avoid vulnerabilities by deleting unused programs and updating software frequently.

4. Mindful Technology Use: Digital downsizing promotes thoughtful technology use. You start to choose your programs, websites, and material more carefully.

Developing a Minimalist Mindset for the Digital Age

1. **"Curate Your Online Presence":** Treat your digital life similarly to your actual things. Keep only what is useful and advances your objectives and interests.

2. **Mindful Media Consumption**: Pay attention to the media you watch. Unfollow people and unsubscribe from publications that don't share your ideals.

3. **Digital Detox**: Disconnect from digital platforms every now and then. Give yourself time to rest and recharge with a digital detox.

4. Plan your digital legacy by deciding which digital possessions you want to leave to loved ones. Include access and management instructions for your online accounts in your estate planning.

Chapter 8 of "The Ultimate Home Downsizing Handbook" discusses how crucial it is to control digital clutter in the present day. Digital clutter can have an impact on our online appearance and mental health in the same way that real goods shape our living spaces. You can achieve a healthy balance between your physical and virtual worlds by using digital shrinking techniques and structuring your digital existence. The advantages are varied, ranging from increased productivity and less stress to a more deliberate and aware use of technology. Remember that the goal of streamlining your digital existence is to create a digital lifestyle that aligns with your beliefs and supports your desire of a simple and fulfilling life as you set out on this path.

Chapter 9

Designing Your New Space

The canvas of your living space presents itself as a blank slate, ready to be filled with intention and purpose as you start the transformational path of downsizing. In Chapter 9 of "The Ultimate Home Downsizing Handbook," we explore the finer points of planning your new home. This chapter is devoted to creating a space that acts as a sanctuary of usefulness and aesthetics while also reflecting your personality and ideals. This chapter walks you through the process of designing a house that fits your downsized lifestyle, from making the most of available space to creating a tapestry of colors and textures.

- Curating Your Environment

1. Assessing Your Needs: Begin by identifying your priorities and needs. What activities can

you accommodate in your space? What kind of habitat do you want to start? The basis for your design journey is this assessment.

2. Creating distinct zones inside your space will help you distinguish between various uses. Set apart spaces for socializing, working, entertainment, and resting.

3. Furniture Selection: Pick pieces that complement your lifestyle and the room. Choose furnishings that are adaptable, multipurpose, and properly proportioned for your smaller home.

4. Integrate nostalgic things into your design to give your room a special sense of purpose. To maintain the coherence of the aesthetic, display them with care.

5. Minimalism and Negative Space: Adopt minimalism by picking your furnishings wisely and letting the empty space breathe. This encourages serenity and reduces clutter.

- Functional and Aesthetic Considerations

1. Flow and Circulation: Make sure that your environment has easy flow and circulation.

Organize the furniture to make it simple to move about and get to different areas.

2. Create a lighting plan that incorporates both natural and artificial lighting. The ambiance is influenced by accent lighting, ambient lighting, and task lighting.

3. Pick a color scheme that works together and establishes the mood for your room. Pops of color bring vibrancy, while neutral tones encourage calm.

4. Introduce different textures and materials to give the scene depth and physical interest. Smooth surfaces should be in harmony with soft textiles and organic materials.

5. Furniture Arrangement: Play around with different furniture configurations until you find the ideal set up. Think on visual harmony, balance, and focal points.

6. To keep your space free of clutter, give practical storage options first priority. Consider furniture with storage options, built-in shelving, and concealed storage.

7. Personalization: Use artwork, furnishings, and accessories to add your distinctive style to the

design. It should feel like a reflection of who you are and where you've been.

Balance between form and function

1. Create functional zones with designated areas for various activities. An effective office, an eating area that is suitable for meals, and a relaxing area that is comfortable are all desirable.

2. Invest in furniture that has multiple uses by buying multifunctional items. You can maximize utility while conserving space by using a wall-mounted workstation, flexible dining table, or sofa bed.

3. Select storage options that can be flexible based on your needs. Adjustable organizers, folding bins, and modular shelving all handle shifting possessions.

4. Flexibility: Consider flexibility when designing. Your area should be flexible enough to change as your demands do. Versatility is provided with mobile furniture, movable walls, and reversible plans.

5. Prioritize ergonomic design for chairs and workstations. Furniture that is supportive and comfortable helps people feel better overall.

Making an aesthetically pleasing haven
1. Maintain a unified look throughout your environment to achieve harmony. This balance creates a sense of unity and aesthetic enjoyment.
2. Nature's Influence: Use natural textures, materials, and indoor plants to include elements of nature. Biophilic architecture improves wellbeing.
3. Select artwork and accessories that speak to you personally. These items add beauty and personality to your home while also telling a narrative.
4. Design spaces for relaxation and awareness for personal retreats. Personal getaways might be created in a relaxing restroom, reading nook, or meditation area.

The process of designing your new space with a careful balance of usefulness and aesthetics is walked you through in Chapter 9 of "The Ultimate Home Downsizing Handbook".

Assessing your needs, establishing zones, and choosing furniture that fits your smaller lifestyle are all parts of curating your environment. Lighting, color, textures, and storage options are all factors that are considered both functionally and aesthetically. Your space will serve your hobbies and reflect your personality thanks to the interaction between form and function.

Remember that your home is a blank canvas for self-expression and mindful living as you set out on this design journey. You may create a sanctuary that supports your wellbeing, fosters your creativity, and encourages your quest of a meaningful and uncluttered life by carefully selecting your environment.

Chapter 10

Transitioning to a Simpler Life

Chapter 10 of "The Ultimate Home Downsizing Handbook" offers advice on the art of transitioning as you begin the significant journey of downsizing and embracing a simpler life. This chapter serves as a link between the idealized picture of your downsized life and the realities of packing up, downsizing, and acclimating to the fulfilling world of a minimalist lifestyle. This chapter gives you the tools you need to seamlessly enter your new chapter, from overcoming the difficulties of moving to developing a mentality that supports intentional living.

- Moving and Settling into a Smaller Space

1. arranging and Organization: Get started by carefully arranging your course of action. Make

a thorough moving checklist that includes details on activities like packing, contacting agencies, and scheduling transportation.

2. Prioritizing Possessions: Before moving, take another look at your belongings. Take into account both what will fit comfortably in your new area and what will actually add value to your life.

3. Adopt a purpose-driven packing strategy via Packing with Purpose. Sort your stuff into groups and carefully label your boxes for simple unpacking.

4. Declutter as You Pack: Keep going with the decluttering process while you pack. Items that no longer fit your smaller lifestyle shouldn't be thrown away or donated.

5. Effective Unpacking: When you get to your new place, unpack with purpose. Organize goods into zones depending on their purpose and requirement.

6. To make the most of your available space, experiment with where you put your furniture. Invest in storage options that fit your new layout perfectly.

- Adjusting to a Minimalist Lifestyle

1. Mindful Consumption: Make it a priority to consume in a mindful manner as the foundation of your minimalist lifestyle. Place an emphasis on quality over quantity and consider the real cost of each transaction.

2. Practice appreciation by being thankful for what you have. Recognize your assets on a regular basis and get rid of everything that is no longer adding to your quality of life.

3. Accept the process of separating yourself from your material possessions. Recognize that experiences and memories are more valuable than things.

4. Reduce digital clutter by applying minimalist ideas to your online activities. De-clutter your digital environments on a regular basis by unfollowing accounts and unsubscribing from communications that no longer benefit you.

5. Focus on Experiences: Shift your attention from acquiring things to acquiring experiences.

Spend money on pursuits that enhance your life and are consistent with your principles.

Navigating Difficulties and Seizing Benefits
1. Be aware that the change to a simpler existence can cause emotional difficulties. As you become used to your new routines and surroundings, be patient with yourself.
2. Address any societal forces that lead people to assemble possessions. Inform others who might not agree with your choice of values and priorities in an appropriate manner.
3. Take advantage of the financial independence that comes with living a simple life. Spending less and paying less for maintenance can enhance savings.
4. Increased Focus: Take note of how clearing your mind of physical and mental clutter leads to an increase in mental clarity and focus. Enjoy your newfound peace of mind.
5. The principles of minimalism are consistent with sustainable living. You may improve the environment and lower your ecological impact by consuming less.

Developing an Attitude of Abundance

1. Perspective Shifting: Adopt the idea of abundance in simplicity. Recognize that the depth of experiences and connections rather than material belongings are the true indicators of a rich life.

2. Allow imperfection to live with your minimalist way of living by Embracing Imperfection. Place more emphasis on making progress than perfecting your path.

3. Assess your goods, obligations, and activities on a regular basis. Make sure they stay in line with your growing values and objectives.

As you make the switch to a simpler existence, Chapter 10 of "The Ultimate Home Downsizing Handbook" represents a turning point. Planning ahead and maximizing available space are essential when downsizing and moving. The mental shift to a minimalist lifestyle is as crucial. This way of living invites you to value experiences above stuff, embrace appreciation, and engage in mindful consumption. Your well-being is enhanced and your financial and environmental consciousness is grown when you successfully navigate the difficulties and embrace the advantages of a minimalist lifestyle. Remember that the idea of a minimalist lifestyle transcends material belongings as you begin this new journey. It's a way of thinking that values purpose, appreciation, and contentment. You can live a life that is meaningful, purposeful, and in line with your inner values by incorporating the ideas of minimalist living into your daily activities.

Chapter 11

Maintaining Your Simplified Lifestyle

In the last chapter of "The Ultimate Home Downsizing Handbook," we discuss the vital skill of upholding the altered, simplified way of life you've worked so hard to create. Chapter 11 serves as a beacon that shows you the way to long-term success in your downsizing endeavors. This chapter discusses tactics that enable you to maintain the deliberate decisions you've made and continue to benefit from your reduced lifestyle. This chapter guarantees that the essence of your downsizing journey remains steady, illuminating your life with simplicity and purpose. It does this by helping you refine your thinking and embrace the delights of clutter-free living.

- Strategies for Long-Term Success

A simple way of living demands continual, deliberate effort to maintain. The following are methods to guarantee long-term success:

1. Evaluate your goods, obligations, and routines on a regular basis. Examine whether they still comport with your scaled-back ideals and objectives.

2. Mindful Consumption: Make fresh purchases with awareness. Before acquiring a new thing to add to your collection, consider how much it will improve your life.

3. Scheduled decluttering is setting out time for recurrent cleaning efforts. To avoid buildup, set aside time at regular intervals to review and adjust your possessions.

4. Extend decluttering to your digital life with these rituals for a digital detox. Create routines for email sorting, file organization, and reducing digital distractions.

5. Experiences are more important than possessions, therefore prioritize them. Spend money on experiences that align with your values and strengthen your bonds.

- Enjoying the Benefits of Downsizing

Downsizing has advantages that go long beyond the initial trip. Enjoy these continuous benefits:

1. Enhanced Well-Being: The absence of physical and mental clutter fosters emotional stability and mental clarity, which in turn fosters a calmer outlook.

2. Freedom of Time: You have more time because you have less possessions to take care of. Put your energy into worthwhile endeavors and activities.

3. A minimalist lifestyle results in fewer maintenance expenses, lower consumption, and more savings, which promotes financial independence.

4. Sustainable Living: Ongoing conscious consumption helps promote a sustainable way of life. You lessen your ecological impact by consuming less.

5. Inner Contentment: Your inner contentment and sense of fulfillment are enriched by living with aim and purpose.

The adventure never ends.

Accept the idea that your quest for a simpler existence is a never-ending adventure.

1. Evolving Values: Be aware that your priorities and values may change over time. Accept change and modify your lifestyle as necessary.

2. Flexibility: Maintain an adaptable mindset. While downsizing is the cornerstone, change your tactics when opportunities and obstacles arise in life.

3. Celebrate Your Progress: Recognize and appreciate Your Success. Every action that leads to a simpler life is a success that should be celebrated.

As you move into a long-term, reduced lifestyle, Chapter 11 of "The Ultimate Home Downsizing Handbook" signals the continuation of your journey. You are equipped to manage your shrunken existence with grace and purpose because of the solutions taught in this chapter. Keep in mind that the true purpose of your trip is creating a conscious, intentional, and joyful way of living as you travel the rewarding route of maintaining a minimalist lifestyle. You uphold the virtues of simplicity with each deliberate decision you make, improve your wellbeing, and leave a legacy of meaning for future generations.

Conclusion

Making a Plan for Simplicity

Your road map for a life-changing path of intentional living has become "The Ultimate Home Downsizing Handbook: What to Save, What to Let Go, and How to Do It with Ease". You started a journey to rethink your relationship with things, places, and the very essence of what defines a home the moment you opened these pages. You've learned through the chapters not only the art of decluttering but also the art of creating a life that reverberates with meaning, joy, and the elegance of simplicity.

Keep in mind that downsizing involves creating space for what is actually important as you consider your journey through the many chapters. Your life will continue to be affected by the lessons you learned from the book, pointing you in the direction of a life that is lighter, more purposeful, and full of opportunities.

You've gained knowledge that will enable you to meet obstacles with grace and savor situations with a fresh appreciation, from changing perceptions and overcoming resistance to embracing the essence of what really important. The ideas you've learned will direct you toward building a sanctuary that reflects your beliefs and promotes your well-being, whether you're curating your environment, dealing with emotional attachments, or developing a new location.

Keep in mind that the trip is not static but rather is always changing as you venture into the world of the minimalist lifestyle. Moving toward a simpler lifestyle is a constant adventure distinguished by self-discovery, mindfulness, and progress rather than an endpoint. Your allies on this ongoing journey will be the long-term success tactics you've acquired and the methods for maintaining your reduced lifestyle.

Downsizing is a thread that connects purpose, intention, and mindfulness in the tapestry of your life. It's a choice to live more deliberately, to value experiences over things, and to appreciate how beautiful each moment is. The advantages of downsizing go beyond the reduction of physical space; they also affect your outlook, your social life, and your relationship with the outside world.

Remember that you have the ability to design a life of significance, depth, and meaning as you move forward. Accept the downsizing's lessons, difficulties, and pleasures as you continue to develop your story. Your journey towards simplicity serves as a source of motivation for both you and those who see the change you've undergone.

The legacy you create via deliberate living should serve as a monument to the remarkable impact that simplicity can have on all facets of your life. May your journey be enlightened by purpose.

About the Author

Beverly J. Shoemake, a seasoned author specializing in parenting and relationships, illuminates the intricate dynamics of human connections. Her insightful narratives inspire growth and resilience in families, offering unique perspectives that foster healthy relationships. With each word, Beverly empowers readers to navigate life's complexities with grace and understanding.

www.ingramcontent.com/pod-product-compliance
Lightning Source LLC
Chambersburg PA
CBHW062331290526
45794CB00005B/1991